PISA TRAVEL GUIDE 2024.

Discover Pisa In 5 Days With Map & Images: Explore The Top Attractions, Best Activities With A Detailed Itinerary & Travel journal, Hotels, Cuisine, Culture & Historical Landmark.

By
BETTY CAULFIELD

Copyright © 2024, Betty Caulfield.

All rights reserved. No part of this publication may be reproduced, distributed, or transmitted in any form or by any means, including photocopying, recording, or other electronic or mechanical methods, without the prior written permission of the publisher, except in the case of brief quotations embodied in critical reviews and certainly other noncommercial uses permitted by copyright law.

Table of Contents

Table of Contents	3
INTRODUCTION	6
Pisa: My Magical Adventure	6
About Pisa	9
Tips for Planning the Best Holiday	11
Crucial Details to Be Aware of Before Traveling to Pisa	14
Pisa Festivals and Celebration	17
The Pisan Time Zone	20
Cost of Travel to Pisa	20
Ways to Get Around Pisa	23
The Best Pisan Neighborhood	26
Pisa's Safety and Emergency Preparedness	29
CHAPTER 1: PISA LOCATIONS WITH STRONG CULTURAL HERITAGE	31
Leaning Tower of Pisa	32
Plaza dei Miracoli	35
San Giovanni Baptistery	42
CHAPTER 2: VISIT THE NATURAL GEMS OF PISA	46
Giardino Scotto	47
San Rossore Natural Park	50
Orto Botanico di Pisa	53
Litorale Pisano	57
CHAPTER 3: 8 PISA HOTELS, RESTAURANTS, MALLS AND BEACHES	61

Hotels	62
Eateries	68
Shopping Centers	75
Amazing Pisa Beaches for the Greatest Water Activities	82
CHAPTER 4: PISA'S FOOD AND DRINKS	85
Pisa's Local and International Cuisine	86
Drink From Pisa And Outside	90
CHAPTER 5: HEALTH, BEAUTY, AND FITNESS	93
Beauty and Spa in Pisa	94
Yoga, Meditation, and Fitness Center in Pisa	100
CHAPTER 6: 3 AND 5-DAY PISA ITINERARY	107
3 Days itinerary plans	107
5-Days Plans for the Vacation	111
CHAPTER 7: PISA'S CAMPING PLANS, ADVICE, AND WEATHER	116
Pisa's Weather Pattern:	117
Some Advice for Pisa Camping	119
Essentials for Camping in Pisa	123
CHAPTER 8: SIMPLE LANGUAGE PHRASES TO KNOW IN PISA	128
Greetings	128
Basic Phrases	128
Asking for Directions	128
Ordering Food and Drinks	129
Making Requests	129
Getting Around	129
Shopping	130
CONCLUSION	131

13 Photography Tips On capturing stunning shots during Pisa Adventure using Smartphone and Digital Camera. 133

TRAVEL JOURNAL 136

Thing to Carry 137

Notes 138

(Friends made and Contact, Cost Calculation) 138

INTRODUCTION

Pisa: My Magical Adventure

My trip to Pisa throughout the years has been an incredible adventure full with experiences captured in the fabric of time. It's about the symphony of experiences sewn into the fabric of my life, not simply about seeing the famous Leaning Tower or the breathtaking Piazza dei Miracoli.

I was enthralled with this Tuscan treasure from the moment I stepped foot there because of its old-world beauty and the way each cobblestone appeared to whisper stories of art and history. The winding lanes took me on a lovely tour through a labyrinth that revealed hidden gems at every turn, whether they were little family-run trattorias serving delicious Tuscan food or secret gelato shops.

But beyond its stunning architecture, Pisa showed me its true spirit via my interactions with its people, whose kindness served as a tribute to the city's unwavering friendliness. In the piazzas, talks flowed easily and the sound of laughing and companionship created a vivid image of a society rich in culture and customs.

Seeing the city's pastel-colored streets became a routine, with every walk offering a chance to take in the tasteful fusion of Renaissance and medieval elements. Pisa's architectural skill and rich tradition were epitomized by the stately Duomo, which was embellished with elaborate artwork, and the Baptistery, which stood proudly next to the famous Leaning Tower.

But it was more than just taking in the sights of the monuments; it was the intangible, the sense of being a part of something eternal, the ambience that reverberated through the majesty of the city's squares and the soft murmurs of the Arno River.

With its sloping magnificence, historical grandeur, and vibrant culture, Pisa became more than just a site to visit; it became a treasured chapter in my trip memoir, a place where the allure of the present blended harmoniously with the beauty of the past.

And when I think back on the years I spent exploring and experiencing Pisa, I bring with me the nostalgia of a magical city that accepted me as one of its own and left a lasting impression on my life's path.

About Pisa

Pisa, a charming city in Tuscany, Italy, is well-known across the globe for its famous leaning tower, but it has much more to offer than just this marvel of architecture. With its magnificent medieval architecture, rich history, and enchanting ambiance, the city is a cultural treasure trove that attracts visitors from all over the world.

Without a doubt, the Leaning Tower of Pisa is one of the main attractions that draw travelers to the city. Its distinctive tilt, the result of an unsteady base, enthralls tourists who are amazed by this technical wonder. The Piazza dei Miracoli, or Square of Miracles, is another popular destination for tourists. It is home to the tower as well as the stunning Pisa Cathedral and Baptistery, which are examples of excellent Romanesque architecture and craftsmanship and are recognized as UNESCO World Heritage Sites.

Beyond the tower, Pisa has plenty to offer in the way of historical and cultural sites. For example, the renowned Scuola Normale Superiore is located in Piazza dei Cavalieri, which was originally the city's political hub in the Middle Ages. The ancient heart of the city offers a beautiful atmosphere for exploring with its cobblestone lanes, medieval buildings, bustling squares, and quaint cafés.

Pisa's charm is further enhanced by the lively local scene, the real Italian food, and the friendly locals. Enjoying authentic Tuscan cuisine and seeing the bustling street markets allows visitors to fully immerse themselves in the local way of life.

All things considered, Pisa's renowned leaning tower is not the only thing that draws visitors; the city's abundance of history, culture, and architectural wonders combine to produce an experience that is memorable in this enchanted Italian city.

Tips for Planning the Best Holiday

Take into account these suggestions to guarantee the greatest trip ever:

1. To minimize last-minute problems, plan ahead by researching your trip, making any required bookings in advance, and creating a flexible schedule.

2. Spend sensibly: Set aside money for lodging, entertainment, food, and mementos. Save a little amount of additional cash for unforeseen costs.

3. Be wise while packing: Take into account the local traditions, the weather, and the activities you have scheduled. Pack light, but don't forget to include essentials like prescriptions, chargers, and crucial papers.

4. Remain adaptable: Although preparation is essential, have an open mind to unplanned events. The greatest moments sometimes come from unanticipated chances.

5. Take part in cultural events, interact with people, and sample the food to fully immerse yourself in the local way of life. This deepens your comprehension of the location and enhances your experience.

6. Strike a balance between exploration and leisure: Take time to relax and enjoy the sights. Give yourself permission to relax and enjoy the trip without feeling hurried.

7. Safety first: Put your health and safety first. Be mindful of your surroundings, observe local regulations, and take all required safety measures.

8. Live in the present and capture memories: While taking pictures and videos can help you remember certain moments, don't forget to put your camera down and take in your surroundings.

9. Experiment: Get out of your comfort zone and try meals or activities you wouldn't often consider. It may bring up pleasant surprises and lifelong memories.

10. Taking care of oneself means paying attention to your body, getting adequate sleep, and drinking enough of water. Because traveling may be exhausting, taking care of oneself is crucial to having a happy trip.

Crucial Details to Be Aware of Before Traveling to Pisa

Requirements for a Visa

- The majority of visitors to Italy need a Schengen visa. Verify the particular visa requirements according to the length of your stay and your country of citizenship. Make sure the validity of your passport is sufficient for the length of your trip.

Traditions & Customs

- Civility and respect are important to Italians. Greetings are vital; popular ways to greet acquaintances are with a handshake and a quick peck on the cheek.
- Wear modest clothing, particularly while visiting places of worship.
Tipping is not required, however it is appreciated at restaurants. Rounding up the bill usually suffices.

Money

- The Euro (€) is Italy's official currency. Prior to your travel, or when you arrive at banks or exchange offices, convert your local money to euros. Although most places take credit cards, it's a good idea to have some cash with you at all times.

Courtesy & Etiquette
- Courtesies and politeness are valued by Italians. "Thank you" (grazie) and "please" (per favore) are very helpful.
- Save your discussions on delicate subjects, such as politics or religion, for intimate companions and suitable environments.

Transportation
- Pisa's transportation network is well-connected. Nearby and easily accessible from the city center is the Pisa Airport.
- Exploring the little city center on foot is highly recommended. In addition, there are railroads, buses, and taxis for transportation.

Language
- The official language is Italian. Although many people are conversant in basic English, it's still beneficial to pick up a few basic Italian words in order to interact and be respectful.

Additional Advice:
- Watch out for pickpockets in popular tourist locations. Make sure your possessions are safe.
- Because the environment might change, check the weather before packing. Although temperatures

might vary, summers can be scorching and winters can be moderate.
- Honor regional traditions, particularly when you visit places of worship. Most of the time, modest attire is required.

Knowing these things before you go to Pisa will improve your trip and make it easier for you to get about the city while honoring the traditions and customs of the locals.

Pisa Festivals and Celebration

Throughout the year, Pisa holds a number of tourist-attracting festivals:

Luminara di San Ranieri: Held on June 16th, this magnificent celebration honors Pisa's patron saint by illuminating the city along the Arno River with thousands of candles.

Gioco del Ponte, or the Battle of the Bridge, is a historical recreation that takes place on the Ponte di Mezzo bridge on the final Saturday in June. It features two teams from the city battling in a medieval-style combat.

Pisa Book Festival: Typically taking place in the fall, this literary gathering of writers, publishers, and book enthusiasts includes readings, debates, and book presentations.

Lucca Comics & Games: Although not in Pisa, the neighboring town of Lucca has one of the largest comic and gaming events in Europe in late October, drawing fans and cosplayers from all over the globe.

Pisa International Film Festival: An yearly occasion that features foreign films and is often hosted in the city over a few months.

For visitors to Pisa, these events provide unique experiences and insights into the local culture.

The Pisan Time Zone

Pisa, Italy is in the Central European Summer Time (CEST) during daylight saving time and the Central European Time (CET) zone during normal time. Whereas CEST is UTC+2, CET is UTC+1. Please be aware that Pisa observes daylight saving time, which causes the clocks to advance by one hour and then regress by one hour, starting on the last Sunday in March and ending on the last Sunday in October.

Cost of Travel to Pisa

Aircraft Flight and Mobility:
- Flight: Depending on the departure location and time of purchase, round-trip airfare to Pisa might vary greatly in price. It might be anything from $300 to $800 or more on average.
- Transportation inside Pisa: A trip on the city's buses or trains might cost anything from $1.50 to $3. Short excursions may cost between $10 and $20 in a taxi.

Accommodation:
- Low-cost lodging: The cost of a hostel or low-cost hotel might vary from $20 to $70 per night.
- Mid-Range Accommodations: The average nightly rate for a hotel may be anything from $80 to $150.

- Luxurious Lodging: Nightly rates at upscale accommodations may vary from $200 to $500 or more.

Dining and Food:
- Budget: $10 to $20 for a basic dinner at a nearby restaurant.
- Mid-Range: Dinners at mid-range establishments may be between $20 and $40 per person.
- Fine Dining: At upmarket places, budget around $50 or more per person.

Activities and Attractions:
- Leaning Tower of Pisa: Entrance to the tower costs around $20, however ticket rates vary.
- Additional Attractions: Entrance fees to museums and galleries range from $5 to $15.

Nightlife and Entertainment:
- Entertainment: Depending on the location and event, prices for things like live music concerts or theatrical shows might go from $10 to $50 or more.
- Nightlife: Drinks at pubs and clubs may cost anywhere from $5 to $15 per, and some may charge admission.

Keep in mind that these are just estimates and may change depending on your personal preferences, travel dates, and other factors. Conducting research and making appropriate plans are wise steps toward efficient budget management.

Ways to Get Around Pisa

Tourists may choose from a number of transportation choices in Pisa, each with an estimated cost:

Walking: The Leaning Tower, Cathedral, and Piazza dei Miracoli are just a few of the major sights in Pisa that are easily accessible by foot from the city center. Walking offers an up-close look at the city's beauty and is free of cost.

Public Bus: CPT (Compagnia Pisana Trasporti) runs an effective bus system in Pisa. You may buy tickets on the bus, in tobacco shops, or from kiosks. A single trip is priced between €1.50 and €2.00 (or €2.50 if purchased aboard) and lasts for seventy minutes.

Renting a bike is a handy and environmentally beneficial way to see Pisa. The price per day for a bike rental might vary, however it usually falls between €10 and €20 depending on the kind of bike and length of rental.

Taxi: The cost of a taxi ride in Pisa varies according on the distance covered. Typically, starting costs fall between €3.50 and €5.00, with extra fees applied every kilometer.

Train: Although they're mostly utilized for interstate travel, trains may also be a useful way to get about the neighborhood. Depending on the location, regional rail tickets within Tuscany may range in price from €5 to €15.

Car Rental: While renting a car offers you more freedom, there are parking fees and possible traffic jams in certain areas of Pisa's historic center. Depending on the kind of automobile, daily car rental costs might vary from €30 to €100+ (without taxes).

When choosing a means of transportation, take convenience and frequency of usage into account. Walking or using public transit may be more cost-effective for shorter distances, but hiring a vehicle may be a good idea for day excursions to neighboring cities or rural exploring.

The Best Pisan Neighborhood

A number of Pisan communities provide a welcoming and secure atmosphere for guests. These are a handful:

San Martino: Piazza dei Miracoli and the Leaning Tower are both nearby. It's secure, well-connected, and has a nice vibe. While prices for lodging in this region might vary, cheap hotels and hostels may cost between $50 and $100 per night.

Another nice and secure area close to the city center is Sant'Antonio, which has easy access to sights and a variety of culinary choices. The cost of lodging may be comparable to that of San Martino.

San Francesco: This neighborhood still offers a welcoming and secure environment, although it is quieter than the city center. The cost of lodging may be comparable to that of the previously listed neighborhoods.

The cost of hotel in these areas varies according to the season, the facilities provided, and the kind of lodging. A more affordable choice could be found in rental flats or Airbnbs, which can range in price from $40 to $150+ per night depending on the location and size.

It's advised to take into account aspects like accessibility to public transit, safety, and individual preferences for the atmosphere and facilities of the area while selecting a place to stay. Travelers to Pisa may often expect a relaxing and safe stay in these areas.

Pisa's Safety and Emergency Preparedness

Emergency Phone Numbers:

In case of a medical emergency, dial 118 to get help.
- Police: To contact the police, dial 112.
- Fire Department: In case of a fire, dial 115.

Insurance

Consider acquiring comprehensive travel insurance that includes repatriation and coverage for medical emergencies.

Health Guard Measures:

- Keep any prescription drugs you may need on hand in their original packaging.
- Drink plenty of water, particularly in the summer, and wear sun protection.

Safety Advice:

- Watch out for pickpockets, particularly in popular tourist locations. Make sure your possessions are safe.
- Honor regional laws and traditions.
- Prior to your journey, keep up with any cautions or warnings about travel.

Being Ready for Emergencies:

Learn the locations of the closest clinics, hospitals, and pharmacies.
- Maintain a list of crucial contacts, such as the Italian embassy or consulate of your nation.
- Be familiar with the emergency protocols of your lodging.

COVID-19 Safety Measures (where relevant):
- Adhere to local health recommendations and laws pertaining to social distance and mask usage.
- During your visit, be aware of any special COVID-19 practices that Pisa may have implemented.

Overall Security:
- Avoid dimly lit locations, particularly after dark.
- Pay attention to traffic lights and use caution while crossing roads.

Keep in mind to use caution and common sense while visiting Pisa. Never hesitate to contact the proper emergency services for assistance in case of an emergency. When traveling, put your health and safety first at all times.

CHAPTER 1: PISA LOCATIONS WITH STRONG CULTURAL HERITAGE

Leaning Tower of Pisa

Location: Piazza dei Miracoli, often known as the Square of Miracles, is where you can find the Leaning Tower of Pisa in Pisa, Italy.

Historical Significance: Its construction started in the 12th century and was intended to serve as a standalone bell tower for the nearby cathedral. The soft ground's instability of the foundation is the reason for the tower's tilt.

Key Features and Draws:
- Architecture: Take in the stunning Romanesque architecture and its recognizable lean.
- View from the Top: For a breathtaking perspective of Pisa, visitors may climb the tower.
- Bells: Discover the background and operation of the bells on the tower.

Guided Tours: For a more educational experience, guided tours are advised and are offered. The tower's surroundings and historical features are discussed by the guides.

Facilities for Visitors: The vicinity of the tower provides visitors with amenities like:
- Lavatories
- Gift stores
- Snack bars and cafés
- Box offices

Crucial Points to Remember:
- Tickets: To prevent lengthy lines, particularly during the busiest travel seasons, it is advised to get tickets in advance.

- Climbing the Tower: Take note that only a certain number of guests may ascend the tower at once. It may not be possible for children under a specific age to climb.

Estimates of Cost:
The cost of an adult ticket to enter the Leaning Tower of Pisa starts at around €18; the price may change depending on the visitor's age and country. There may be extra fees associated with guided tours.
- Guided Tours: Depending on the length of the tour and the contents, guided tours may cost anywhere from €10 and €25 per person.

Make a plan and think about buying tickets online or from reliable tour companies. Remember that going to the tower is a well-liked tourist destination in Pisa, so making reservations in advance will help control expenses and guarantee availability.

Plaza dei Miracoli

Location: Known for its historical and architectural importance, Piazza dei Miracoli is situated in the center of Pisa, Italy.

Historical Significance: The plaza is home to four major religious sites and is recognized as a UNESCO World Heritage Site.

- Pisa's Leaning Tower
- The Duomo di Pisa, or the Pisa Cathedral
- San Giovanni Baptistery (Battistero di San Giovanni)
- The Monumental Cemetery at Camposanto

Key Features and Draws:
The Pisa Cathedral, with its elaborate decorations and exquisite artwork, is a magnificent example of Romanesque architecture.
- Baptistery of St. John: renowned for its elaborate architecture and superb acoustics.
- Camposanto Monumentale: An old cemetery including magnificent statues and murals.
- Leaning Tower of Pisa: A prominent feature of the plaza is this famous tower, which is named for its lean.

Guided Tours: To fully understand the historical and cultural importance of the plaza and its monuments, guided tours are offered and strongly advised. Skilled tour guides provide information about the history, design, and narratives of these iconic sites.

Visitor Amenities: The square provides a range of amenities for guests, such as:
- Points of sale for admission to monuments

- Lavatories
- Information hubs
- Gift stores
- Snack bars and cafés

Crucial Points to Remember:
- Tickets: Generally, you need a separate ticket to enter each monument at Piazza dei Miracoli. There may be affordable combo tickets available for visiting many monuments.
- Crowds: The plaza may become quite busy during the busiest travel seasons. If you want to avoid standing in line, try going early in the day.

Estimates of Cost:
- Ticket Prices: Admission fees to individual monuments range from €5 to €20. Purchasing combination tickets for many monuments may result in discounts.
- Guided Tours: Depending on the length and inclusions, guided tours of the plaza and its monuments may cost anywhere from €10 to €30 or more per person.

Touring Piazza dei Miracoli provides an enthralling excursion through the architectural wonders and rich history of Pisa. Organizing ahead of time, thinking about combination tickets, and choosing guided tours are ways to improve the experience and save money.

Duomo di Pisa

Location: The Duomo di Pisa, or Pisa Cathedral, is located in Piazza dei Miracoli, or the Square of Miracles, in Pisa, Italy.

35

Historical Significance: Constructed throughout the 11th and 12th centuries, the cathedral is a prominent religious and cultural monument in Pisa and a masterwork of Romanesque design.

Key Features and Draws:
- Architecture: With its marble front, elaborate sculptures, and ornate columns, the cathedral exhibits exquisite Romanesque architecture.
- Interior Artwork: Take in the exquisite murals, mosaics, and a spectacular pulpit created by Giovanni Pisano, among other works of art.
- Giovanni Pisano's Pulpit: Known for its superb workmanship, this finely carved pulpit is a standout.

Guided Tours: For a more in-depth understanding of the Pisa Cathedral's history, architecture, and the importance of its artwork, guided tours are offered and highly recommended.

Visitor Facilities: Some of the amenities offered to guests are as follows:
- Entry ticket offices
- Optional guided tours or audio guides
- Lavatories
- Information tables
- Souvenir stores selling gifts

Crucial Points to Remember:
- Tickets: You may buy admission tickets to the Pisa Cathedral independently or as part of a combo ticket that grants you entry to the Piazza dei Miracoli's many monuments.
- Clothing Code: Visitors are asked to dress modestly, covering their knees and shoulders, as they do at many Italian holy sites.

Estimates of Cost:
- Ticket Prices: Depending on age and country, entry tickets to the Pisa Cathedral may cost anything from €5 to €10 per person. Purchasing combination tickets for many monuments may result in discounts.
- Guided Tours: Depending on the length and inclusions, guided tours of the cathedral may cost anything from €10 to €20 or more per person.

When exploring the Pisa Cathedral, tourists may take in its creative riches and architectural magnificence together with its religious and historical importance. To improve your experience, think about buying tickets in advance or choosing guided excursions.

San Giovanni Baptistery

Location: The Baptistery of St. John lies next to the Pisa Cathedral in Piazza dei Miracoli, or the Square of Miracles, in Pisa, Italy.

Historical Significance: The Baptistery, one of Pisa's oldest structures, is recognized for both its remarkable architectural design and historical significance. It was constructed in the 12th and 13th centuries.

Key Features and Draws:
- Architecture: The Baptistery's façade and interior are adorned with elaborate decorations that combine Gothic and Romanesque architectural motifs.
- Pulpit and Interior Design: Take in the exquisite interior details, including ornamental pieces and artwork, as well as the beautifully carved pulpit.
- Acoustics: Take in the Baptistery's superb acoustics, which accentuate musical performances.

Guided Tours: To get an understanding of the Baptistery's importance, history, and architecture, guided tours are offered.

Facilities for Visitors: Offerings to guests include:
- Entry ticket counters
- Optional guided tours or audio guides
- Lavatories
- Information tables
- Gift stores

Crucial Points to Remember:

- Tickets: You may buy admission tickets to the Baptistery independently or in combination with other tickets to get entry to many monuments in Piazza dei Miracoli.
- Acoustics and Performances: Try to catch a musical act, or just clap or listen for echoes within the Baptistery to enjoy the acoustics.

Estimates of Cost:

- Ticket Prices: Depending on age and country, entry tickets to the Baptistery might cost anywhere from €5 to €10 per person. Purchasing combination tickets for many monuments may result in discounts.
- Guided Tours: Depending on the length and inclusions, guided tours of the Baptistery may cost anywhere from €10 to €20 or more per person.

Travelers may experience Pisa's rich cultural legacy while admiring the Baptistery of St. John's architectural beauty, historical relevance, and auditory miracles. When planning your visit to Piazza dei Miracoli, think about putting it in your schedule.

CHAPTER 2: VISIT THE NATURAL GEMS OF PISA

Giardino Scotto

Location: Giardino Scotto is situated close to Pisa's old town on the banks of the Arno River in Italy.

Historical Significance: The garden was first built as a defensive fortification in the fourteenth century. It evolved into a public garden throughout time, offering both residents and tourists a tranquil haven.

Key Features and Draws:
- Scenic Riverside Views: The Arno River and its environs are beautifully visible to visitors.
- Green Spaces: The garden has paths, serene spots to unwind in, and well-kept vegetation.
- Outdoor activities: Occasionally holds concerts, exhibits, or other cultural activities that liven up the atmosphere.

Guided Tours: Giardino Scotto does not usually provide official guided tours. The garden is open for visitors to explore at their leisure.

Facilities for Visitors:
- Restrooms: There may be amenities close by.
- Picnic areas and benches: Great for unwinding and taking in the scenery.
- Playground: There may be kid-friendly play places scattered around the garden.
- Occasional Events: To learn about any events or activities taking place in the garden, check the local listings.

Crucial Points to Remember:

- Accessibility: The garden is normally free to enter and is available to the general public.
- Opening Hours: It's best to verify ahead of time since the hours may change depending on the season.
- Crowds: On weekends or during major events, it may become busy depending on the season.

Estimated Cost: Admission to Giardino Scotto is often free for the general public. If any particular exhibits or activities are conducted in the garden, there can be additional entrance costs.

Travelers may rest in the peace and quiet of nature and take in the gorgeous views along the Arno River by visiting Giardino Scotto, which provides a serene diversion from the busy attractions of the city.

San Rossore Natural Park

Location: San Rossore Nature Park is close to Pisa and spans a portion of the Arno River delta as well as a coastal region.

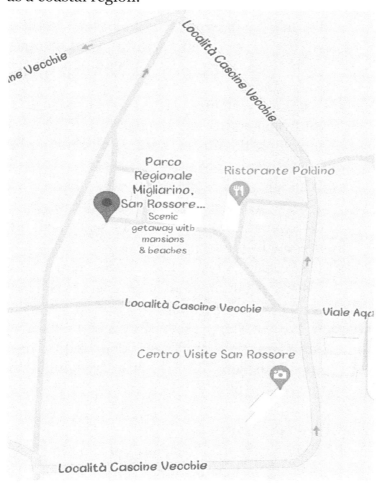

Historical value: The park's multiple ecosystems, which act as a protected area to preserve a range of habitats and species, give it historical value.

Key Features and Draws:
- Diverse Landscapes: The San Rossore Nature Park is home to a variety of habitats, such as meadows, marshlands, and woodlands.
- Wildlife Watching: It's a great place for birdwatchers to see a range of bird species, including flamingos, herons, and numerous migrating birds.
- Walking and Cycling Trails: There are several paths in the park that allow you to discover the natural splendor while walking, cycling, or horseback riding.
- Historical Sites: The park may have historical buildings in some regions, such as farms and rural homes.

Guided Tours: The park's visitor center or nearby tour companies may provide guided tours. These trips provide insights into the history, fauna, and ecosystems of the park.

Facilities for Visitors:
- Visitor Centers: These are information hubs offering park maps, tours, and details.

- Restrooms: The park has facilities at certain locations.
- Picnic Areas: Set aside locations for leisurely strolls and picnics.
- Bike Rentals: If you want to explore the trails on a bike, certain locations may rent bikes.

Crucial Points to Remember:
- Entrance price: Normally, entering the park may incur a small price. Certain sections of the park, age groups, and nationalities may all have different prices.
- Opening Hours: For information on opening hours, including any seasonal changes, see the park's official website or visitor centers.
- Guided Tours: During popular seasons, reservations may be required in advance for guided tours.
-

Cost Estimate: Depending on age, group rates, and the portions of the park that are accessible, admission prices at San Rossore Nature Park may vary from €2 to €10 per person.

Nature enthusiasts have a great chance to explore a variety of landscapes, see animals, engage in outdoor sports, and take in the stunning natural surroundings at San Rossore Nature Park, all close to Pisa.

Orto Botanico di Pisa

Location: The Orto Botanico di Pisa, often known as the Botanical Garden of Pisa, is situated close to the University of Pisa in the Italian city of Pisa.

Historical Significance: The garden, which was founded in 1544, is among the world's oldest botanical gardens and has a significant historical bearing on botany and scientific study.

Key Features and Draws:
- Botanical Diversity: A large range of plant species, including exotic trees, medicinal plants, and a collection of cacti and succulents, are housed in the garden.
- Historical Greenhouses: Featuring rare and unusual plant species, visitors may tour historical greenhouses.
- Educational Tours: With its emphasis on plant biology, conservation, and historical relevance, the garden provides educational experiences.

Tours with Guides: For anyone interested in learning more about the history, plant collections, and current research of the garden, guided tours are offered and strongly advised.

Facilities for Visitors:
- Visitor Center: Schedules for guided tours, maps, and historical details about the garden.

- instructional Resources: Certain locations may offer tourists exhibitions or instructional resources.
- Restrooms: There are restrooms within or next to the garden.
- Gift stores: A few gardens may contain gift stores with souvenirs featuring plants.

Crucial Points to Remember:
- Guided Tours: Verify the availability and scheduling of guided tours ahead of time.
- Photography: Adhere to any rules that may be in place when it comes to taking pictures or handling plants.
- Accessibility: Wheelchair users and others with restricted mobility may find walkways in the garden appropriate.

Estimated Cost: Entrance costs at the Pisan Botanical Garden may vary from €3 to €8 per person, with further savings available for elderly, students, and groups. There may be extra fees for guided excursions, which usually range from €5 to €15 per person.Exploring a variety of plant collections, learning about botanical research, and taking in the beauty of nature in a historically significant environment are all made possible by a visit to the Botanical Garden of Pisa.

Litorale Pisano

Location: The Tyrrhenian Sea shore in the Tuscany area, close to Pisa, Italy, is known as the Litorale Pisano.

Historical Significance: The coastline is renowned for its beaches and natural beauty, but it has also played a significant role in the region's commerce and marine operations.

Key Features and Draws:
- Beaches: There are a number of sandy beaches along the coast, such as Marina di Pisa, Tirrenia, and Calambrone, where visitors may swim and sunbathe.
- Seafront Promenades: Take leisurely walks along these waterfront promenades, which are dotted with eateries, cafés, and stores selling regional fare and trinkets.
- Water Sports: Because of the ideal wind conditions along the coastline, sports like sailing, windsurfing, and kiteboarding are quite popular.
- Natural Reserves: Certain regions may have protected areas with dunes and coastal habitats, often known as natural reserves.

Guided trips: For some activities, like as water sports or touring neighboring nature reserves, guided trips around the coastline may be offered. Some services may be provided by nearby tour companies.

Facilities for Visitors:
- Beach Facilities: Depending on the beach, amenities may include loungers, umbrellas for hire, showers, and bathrooms.

- Water Sports Equipment Rental: A few locations provide water sports equipment rentals.
- Restaurants and Cafés: There are many places to eat along the shore where you may sample regional seafood meals and drinks.

Crucial Points to Remember:
Seasonal Variation: During the summer (June to August), there may be a greater availability of beach amenities and activities.
- Crowds: During the busiest travel seasons, popular beaches may become crowded, so getting there early may help you snag a place.

Estimated Cost: Public beaches along the Pisan coast are usually free to access. Nevertheless, there may be fees for things like renting beach chairs, parasols, water sport gear, and eating at seaside eateries.

Discovering the Litorale Pisano gives visitors the opportunity to unwind on gorgeous beaches, partake in a variety of activities, and take in the allure of the Tyrrhenian Sea coastline close to Pisa.

CHAPTER 3: 8 PISA HOTELS, RESTAURANTS, MALLS AND BEACHES

Hotels

Low-cost Hotels:

1. The Bologna Hotel
- Description: This hotel, which is close to Pisa Centrale Train Station, provides straightforward yet cozy accommodations with standard facilities. It offers a pleasant stay at a reasonable cost and convenient access to the city's attractions.
Location: 56125 Pisa PI, Italy; Via Giuseppe Mazzini, 57
- Estimated Cost: Rates for a night's stay typically vary from $50 to $80.

2. The Hotel Terminus & Plaza
- Description: This motel offers clean, basic lodging close to the train station and the Leaning Tower, both of which are accessible by foot. For guests on a tight budget who yet want to be close to important sites, it's a good option.
- Address: 77 Giovanni Amendola Street, 56125 Pisa, Italy
- Estimated Cost: Nightly rates often fall between $60 and $90.

3. Moderno Hotel
- Description: Located in the heart of Pisa, Hotel Moderno provides simple accommodations in a

handy position among the city's attractions. For those on a tight budget, it offers a cozy stay at affordable prices.

The address is 103, Via F. Corridoni, 56125 Pisa PI, Italy.

- Estimated Cost: Nightly rates range from around $70 to $100.

4. Alessandro della Spina Hotel

- Description: This motel offers reasonably priced and cozy accommodations close to the train station. It accommodates budget guests and provides convenient access to transit and sights.

Via Alessandro Della Spina, 5, 56125 Pisa PI, Italy is the address.

- Estimated Cost: Nightly rates vary from around $80 to $110.

Mid-Priced Accommodations:

1. Relais Dell'Orologio Hotel

- Description: This hotel, located next to the Leaning Tower in a historic structure, provides tastefully decorated rooms with high-end services. For tourists looking for a little elegance, it offers an opulent yet fairly priced stay.

- Address: 12–14 Via della Faggiola, 56126 Pisa PI, Italy

- Estimated Cost: Nightly rates often fall between $120 and $180.

2. NH Pisa
- Description: The NH Pisa offers contemporary, cozy accommodations with first-rate amenities close to the Pisa Centrale Train Station. It provides reasonable costs for high-quality service and convenience.
Piazza della Stazione, 2, 56125 Pisa PI, Italy is the address.
- Estimated Cost: Nightly rates range from around $100 to $150.

3. The Marriott Pisa AC Hotel
- Description: Conveniently situated close to the airport, this modern hotel provides chic accommodations with all the comforts of home. It guarantees that visitors will have a good time and suits mid-range budgets.
- Address: 20 Via dell'Ostrucci, 56124 Pisa PI, Italy
- Estimated Cost: Nightly rates vary from around $110 to $160.

4. Hotel Marinara Repubblica
- Description: This hotel offers nice amenities and big rooms, situated a short distance from the city

center. It provides a good mix of comfort and cost, making it ideal for tourists on a moderate budget.
- Address: 81 Via Matteucci Andrea, 56124 Pisa, Italy
- Estimated Cost: Nightly rates range from around $90 to $130.

Luxurious Hotels:
1. Luxurious Hotel Duomo
- Description: This upmarket hotel, which is adjacent to the Leaning Tower, has opulent accommodations with expansive views. With elegant facilities, it offers a first-rate experience.
- Address: 94 Santa Maria Avenue, 56126 Pisa, Italy
- Estimated Cost: Nightly rates vary from $180 to $250.

2. The Fiori Report
- Description: This boutique hotel in the center of Pisa provides tasteful accommodations and attentive service. It offers a sumptuous stay that is comfortable and well designed.
Via Cardinale Maffi, 9, 56127 Pisa PI, Italy is the address.
- Estimated Cost: Nightly rates range from $200 to $300.

3. Bagni di Pisa
- Description: Situated just outside of Pisa, this opulent hotel provides tranquil surroundings and spa services. It offers a sumptuous hideaway with spa facilities.
Largo Shelley, 18, 56017 San Giuliano Terme PI, Italy is the address.
- Estimated Cost: Nightly rates vary from $250 to $400.

4. The Hotel Pisa Tower
- Description: This opulent hotel provides elegant lodging and is conveniently close to the Leaning Tower. It offers a posh experience with an emphasis on superior customer care.
Via Andrea Pisano, 23, 56122 Pisa PI, Italy is the address.
- Estimated Cost: Nightly rates range from around $220 to $300.

Please be aware that the price ranges given are approximations and may change depending on the time of year, the availability of rooms, and the dates of the reservation.

Eateries

Restaurants on a Budget:
1. La Tana d'Orso
- Description: This trattoria, which is close to the Leaning Tower, serves excellent Tuscan food at affordable costs. Traditional fare like pizza and spaghetti is served, along with regional delicacies.

- Address: 71 Santa Maria Avenue, 56126 Pisa, Italy
- Estimated Cost: The price per person ranges from €8 to €15.

2. Cavelieria Osteria
- Description: This welcoming restaurant offers real Italian food and wines in the heart of the historic district. It has a menu that highlights local food together with a warm, inviting ambiance.
- Address: 16 San Frediano Street, 56126 Pisa, Italy
- Estimated Cost: Usually between €15 and €25 per person.

3. The Olsteino
- Description: Located close to the Arno River, this reasonably priced eatery serves a selection of pizzas and classic Italian fare. It's a laid-back location with patio furniture.
Lungarno Antonio Pacinotti, 19, 56126 Pisa PI, Italy is the address.
- Estimated Cost: Generally, each passenger pays between €10 and €18.

4. Il Montino
- Description: This family-owned eatery in the city center serves hearty Italian fare at reasonable costs. It's well-known for its tasty food and welcoming service.

- Address: 180 Via Santa Maria, 56126 Pisa, Italy
- Estimated Cost: The price per person ranges from €10 to €20.

Mid-Priced Dining Establishments:
1. Galileo Restaurant
- Description: Serving seafood and Tuscan delights, this restaurant is situated close to the Leaning Tower. It offers a classy eating experience that emphasizes regional cuisine.
- Address: 115 Via Santa Maria, 56126 Pisa, Italy
- Estimated Cost: The price per person ranges from €20 to €35.

2. Pizza Restaurant Da Gennaro
- Description: Located in the heart of the city, this restaurant serves classic Italian cuisine and a wide selection of pizzas. It's a laid-back restaurant with good meals served in a casual atmosphere.
- Address: 167 Via Santa Maria, 56126 Pisa, Italy
- Estimated Cost: Usually between €15 and €30 per person.

3. La Grotta dell'Anno
- Description: Located close to the Arno River, this eatery specializes on Tuscan cooking using seasonal, locally sourced ingredients. It has a varied food together with a warm atmosphere.

The address is 22 Lungarno Mediceo, 56126 Pisa PI, Italy.
- Estimated Cost: The price per person ranges from €25 to €40.

4. Alla Bandiera Restaurant
- Description: Located in the center of Pisa, this eatery serves Italian and Tuscan cuisine on a varied menu. It offers delicious meals and a welcoming eating environment.
The address is 74 Via S. Martino, 56125 Pisa PI, Italy.
- Price Estimate: The average cost per person is between €30 and €45.

Luxurious Dining Establishments:

1. Gourmet Restaurant Galileo

- Description: This elegant restaurant, which serves gourmet dining with an emphasis on Tuscan food, is close to the Leaning Tower. It serves gourmet food in an opulent atmosphere.
- Address: 94 Santa Maria Avenue, 56126 Pisa, Italy
- Estimated Cost: The price per person ranges from €50 to €80.

2. Restoring the Tuscan

- Description: This classy eatery with a focus on Tuscan and Italian cuisine is located in the historic center. It provides a classy, meticulous eating experience.
Location: 55, 56100 Pisa PI, Italy's Via Giuseppe Garibaldi
- Estimated Cost: The starting price per person is between €60 and €100.

3. La Buca di San Antonio
Situated in Piazza dei Cavalieri, this well-known eatery offers sophisticated Tuscan fare. It is renowned for its fine dining and premium ingredients.
Via Santa Giusta, 5, 56126 Pisa PI, Italy is the address.

- Estimated Cost: The price per person ranges from €70 to €120.

4. Restoring the dependable Marinare
- Description: Slightly out from the city core, this upscale eatery offers inventive cuisine emphasizing premium ingredients. It offers a classy eating experience.
- Address: 81 Via Matteucci Andrea, 56124 Pisa, Italy
- Estimated Cost: Generally, prices begin at

€80–€150 for each individual.

Please be aware that the prices shown are approximations and may change depending on the food and beverages selected as well as the particular menu items offered by the restaurant.

Shopping Centers

Although Pisa lacks conventional big retail facilities like malls, there are a number of shopping neighborhoods and locations that may accommodate a range of spending limits and tastes:

Shopping Destinations - Low Cost:
1. Italy's Cup:
- Description: A bustling retail district with a variety of boutiques, local businesses, and shops providing reasonably priced apparel, accessories, and mementos. It's perfect for thrifty shopping.
- Address: 56125 Pisa PI, Italy; Corso Italia
- Estimated Cost: Items often fall within the affordable range of €10 to €50, however prices do vary.

2. Borgo Stretto:
- Description: Shops offering clothes, handmade items, and regional specialties may be found in Borgo Stretto, which is renowned for its winding lanes and little boutiques. It is appropriate for consumers on a tight budget.
Location: 56127 Pisa PI, Italy; Borgo Stretto
- Estimated Cost: The cost of the products ranges from €15 to €80.

3. The Square of the Vettovaglie:

- Description: During the day, a lively market in the plaza with fresh food, regional goods, and handcrafted things is held. Items that are affordable for visitors include fruits, veggies, and mementos.
- Address: Piazza delle Vettovaglie, Pisa, Italy, 56126
- Estimated Cost: Though prices vary, local goods and fresh fruit are fairly priced, with prices beginning at a few euros.

4. The market for pulses:
- Description: Also known as the flea market, this place is ideal for those looking to score cheap antiques, rare bargains, and used goods.
- Address: Vittorio Emanuele II Piazza, 56125 Pisa PI, Italy
- Estimated Cost: A few of the goods have beginning costs as low as €5, making them affordable.

Mid-Size Budget:
1. Corso Matteotti:
- Description: Corso Matteotti provides a wide choice of clothes, shoes, and accessories at reasonable costs, with a focus on mid-range brands and boutiques.
Location: 56127 Pisa PI, Italy; Corso Matteotti
- Estimated Cost: Clothes and accessories usually cost between €30 to €150, while exact prices vary.

2. Through Santa Maria:
- Description: A variety of shops and boutiques offering apparel, accessories, and handcrafted goods can be found on this street. It provides a combination of more expensive and less expensive things, catering to mid-range budgets.
- Address: Santa Maria Avenue, 56126 Pisa, Italy
- Approximate Cost: The price range for apparel and accessories is €40 to €200.

3. Garibaldi Square:
- Description: Piazza Garibaldi, well-known for its neighborhood stores and marketplaces, provides a selection of traditional goods, apparel, and accessories at reasonable costs.
- Address: 56127 Pisa PI, Italy; Piazza Garibaldi
- Estimated Cost: Though prices vary, most goods fall between €30 and €120.

4. The New Market in Pisa:
- Description: Also referred to as the New Market, this lively neighborhood is home to a number of stores that provide a range of products, such as apparel, accessories, and trinkets. It suits those with moderate budgets.
- Location: 56126 Pisa PI, Italy, Via Guglielmo Oberdan

- Estimated Cost: Although item prices vary, they typically range from €20 to €100.

Shopping Districts - Luxurious:
1. The Cavalieri Plaza:
- Description: Exquisite shops and designer businesses offering upscale apparel, accessories, and jewelry at premium pricing can be found in this exquisite plaza.
Location: 56126 Pisa PI, Italy; Piazza dei Cavalieri

- Estimated Cost: Although the cost of luxury goods varies greatly, it typically starts at €200 and may reach several thousand dollars.

2. Corso Italia (Premium Stores):
- Description: Although Corso Italia has shops for every budget, it also has a few upscale boutiques and designer businesses that sell high-end goods at premium costs.
- Address: 56125 Pisa PI, Italy; Corso Italia
- Estimated Cost: Designer products might cost anywhere from €300 to €3000 or more.

3. Santa Maria Avenue (Upmarket Stores):
- Description: Via Santa Maria is home to a number of upscale boutiques and designer outlets that sell expensive apparel, accessories, and other items in addition to its mid-range retailers.
- Address: Santa Maria Avenue, 56126 Pisa, Italy
- Estimated Cost: Although the cost of luxury goods varies greatly, it usually starts at €400 and may go considerably higher.

4. Street San Martino:
- Description: High-end designer labels and luxury goods with steep price tags may be found in this neighborhood's boutiques and specialized shops.
- Address: San Martino Street, Pisa, Italy, 56127

- Estimated Cost: The starting price for luxury products is €500, and the price goes up considerably for high-end designer things.

Note that the prices shown are approximations and may vary considerably depending on the particular products, brands, and in-store specials that apply at the time of purchase.

Amazing Pisa Beaches for the Greatest Water Activities

Low-cost Beaches:

1. Beach at Marina di Pisa:
- Location: Along the shoreline south of Pisa.
- About: A free, sandy beach with cafés and restaurants along it, affording views of the Tyrrhenian Sea.
- Water Sports: beach volleyball, swimming, and tanning.
- Estimated Cost: Free admission; small fees for beach chairs and umbrellas, if available for rent.

2. Beach Tirrenia:
Location: Close to Calambrone, south of Pisa.
- About: A long, sandy beach with both free and paid portions, as well as public spaces and beach clubs.
- Water Sports: paddleboarding, windsurfing, and swimming.
- Estimated Cost: Free admission to public spaces, fees for renting gear or to exclusive beach clubs.

Beaches with Mid-Range Budgets:

3. Beach Calambrone:
- Location: Known for its excellent sandy coastlines, south of Pisa.

- About: A clean, well-kept beach featuring areas for free and others that need payment, complete with water activities, loungers, and umbrellas.
- Water Sports: beach volleyball, kiteboarding, and surfing.
- Estimated Cost: Some sites are free to enter; services and equipment must be rented.

4. Beach at Marina di Vecchiano:
- Location: Near Vecchiano, north of Pisa.
- About: A natural, less congested beach that offers a laid-back atmosphere with both free and paid beach clubs.
- Water Sports: fishing, swimming, and snorkeling.
- Estimated Cost: No admission fees for public spaces; fees for beach club use or rentals.

Luxurious Beaches:
5. Pisa Bagno Vittorio Beach Marina:
The location is at Pisa's Marina.
- About: A fully furnished beach club with umbrellas, lounge chairs, and a variety of amenities including eateries and bars.
- Water Sports: Jet skiing, water skiing, banana boat excursions.
- Estimated Cost: Admission fee or fees for used facilities and services.

6. Bagno Calambrone Europa Beach:
- Location: Near Calambrone.
- About: A chic beach club with a classy atmosphere that offers top-notch services, fine loungers, dining options, and bars.
- Water Activities: Private beach parties, sailing, and luxury boat rentals.
Cost Estimate: Increased admission prices or out-of-pocket costs for deluxe services.

Take note:
Depending on the beach, the time of year, and the services offered, costs for beach amenities including loungers, umbrellas, and water sports gear may vary from €5 to €20 or more per item or activity. While some beaches charge an admission fee for private facilities, others may offer free public sections with paid services.

CHAPTER 4: PISA'S FOOD AND DRINKS

Pisa's Local and International Cuisine

Regional foods

1. Rice Torte from Pisa (Torta co' bischeri):
- Description: A savory rice cake piled with salami or prosciutto, prepared with rice, eggs, and Parmesan cheese.
- Estimated Cost: At nearby restaurants, servings often cost between €8 and €15.

2. Cecina:
- Description: A thin, crispy flatbread-like pancake made from chickpea flour and seasoned with olive oil and rosemary.
- Estimated Cost: From neighborhood bakeries or street sellers, they typically cost between €3 and €6 per piece.

3. Aquacotta Soup:
- Description: A classic vegetable soup that's often topped with a poached egg and cooked with tomatoes, onions, garlic, and other vegetables.
- Estimated Cost: At neighborhood trattorias and eateries, servings typically cost between €8 and €12.

4. Cinghiale alla Cacciatora, or stew of wild boar:

- Description: A Tuscan delicacy, slow-cooked wild boar simmered in tomatoes, red wine, and fragrant herbs.
- Estimated Cost: While prices in restaurants might vary, they usually range from €15 to €25 per dish.

Foreign Cuisines:
1. Margherita pizza:
- Description: A traditional Italian pizza with fresh basil, mozzarella cheese, tomato sauce, and olive oil on top.
- Estimated Cost: A small to medium-sized pizza costs between €6 and €12.

2. sushi
- Description: Sushi rolls come in a variety of forms, such as maki, nigiri, and sashimi, and they're often served with wasabi and soy sauce.
- Cost Estimate: In Japanese restaurants, a set or platter typically costs between €10 and €20. However, prices might vary.

3. Kebab
- Description: Middle Eastern-style grilled meat, usually lamb or chicken, wrapped on flatbread and accompanied by veggies, sauces, and condiments.
- Estimated Cost: A kebab sandwich or wrap costs between €5 and €8.

4. Carbonara pasta:
- Description: Pancetta, eggs, Pecorino Romano cheese, spaghetti, and black pepper are combined to make this Italian pasta dish.
- Estimated Cost: While prices in Italian restaurants vary, they typically range from €8 to €15 per dish.

Please be aware that the prices shown are approximations and may change based on the location, degree of service, and quality of the products used in the restaurant.

Drink From Pisa And Outside

Regional Drinks:

1. Chianti Wine:
- Description: A well-known Tuscan wine, especially from the Chianti area, that goes well with Italian food because of its fruity taste, rich red color, and adaptability.
- Estimated Cost: In local stores or restaurants, bottles range in price from €10 to €30, depending on brand and quality.

2. Vin Santo:
- Description: Traditionally served with cantucci, or almond cookies, for dipping, this sweet dessert wine is prepared from dried grapes.
- Cost Estimate: Depending on the manufacturer and aging method, bottles might cost anywhere from €15 to €40.

3. Limoncello
- Description: Traditionally served as a digestif, this lemon liqueur is produced by steeping lemon zest in alcohol. It tastes zesty and invigorating.
- Estimated Cost: Depending on brand and quality, 500ml bottles range in price from €15 to €20.

4. Grappa:
- Description: Remaining grape pomace from winemaking is used to make this potent alcoholic beverage. It may be used as a digestive and is available in a variety of tastes.
- Estimated Cost: Depending on age and quality, prices may vary significantly, usually between €20 and €60 per bottle.

Foreign Drinks:
1. Prosecco
- Description: A popular ingredient in Bellini drinks and a favorite on its own, this Italian sparkling wine has a crisp, light flavor.
- Estimated Cost: Depending on the brand and quality, bottles might cost anywhere from €8 to €20.

2. Tonic and Gin:
- Description: A traditional mixed cocktail with lime garnish with gin and tonic water. It's a well-liked option at eateries and pubs.
- Estimated Cost: Drinks range in price from €7 to €15, depending on the kind of gin used.

3. Whiskey (Bourbon, Irish, Scotch):

- Description: A variety of whiskeys with distinct tastes and manufacturing processes that come from Scotland, Ireland, or the United States.
- Cost Estimate: Depending on the brand, quality, and age, prices may vary greatly; luxury types might cost several hundred euros each bottle, while regular prices start at €20.

4. Mojito:
- Description: A zesty and delightful drink with lime juice, sugar, mint leaves, white rum, and soda water.
- Estimated Cost: Drinks in pubs and restaurants often cost between €7 and €15.

Please be aware that the costs shown are approximations and may vary depending on the location, kind of venue (restaurant or bar), and brand or quality of beverage.

CHAPTER 5: HEALTH, BEAUTY, AND FITNESS

Beauty and Spa in Pisa

Low Budget

1. Benessere Pisa Center
- Description: At reasonable prices, this facility provides basic spa services including massages, facials, and wellness treatments.
Via Nicola Pisano, 8, 56127 Pisa PI, Italy is the address.
- Estimated Cost: Depending on the procedure, service costs might range from €20 to €50.

2. The Lilla Cipria Beauty
- Description: An affordable beauty shop providing pedicures, manicures, and skincare services.
The address is 67 Via San Martino, 56125 Pisa PI, Italy.
- Estimated Cost: Although servicing costs vary, they often range from €15 to €40.

3. Benessere Club
- Description: This institution offers body treatments and massages at reasonable prices.
- Address: Luigi Bianchi Avenue, 34, Pisa, Italy 56121
- Estimated Cost: The normal price range for different procedures is between €25 and €60.

4. Bellezza Divina

- Description: Provides affordable beauty treatments, such as manicures, pedicures, and waxing.

The address is 26 Via Sant'Antonio, 56124 Pisa PI, Italy.

- Estimated Cost: Services range in price from €15 to €35.

5. Area In Forma

- Description: Offers affordable spa and fitness services, such as massages and exercise programs.

Via Francesco Traniello, 31, 56121 Pisa PI, Italy is the address.

- Estimated Cost: Depending on the service, prices might vary, but they often begin around €20.

Mid-Range Affordable Beauty and Spa:

1. SPA Pisa - Point of Beauty

- Description: Reasonably priced spa services like body treatments, facials, and massages are available.

Place of business: 43 Via Mario Giuntini, 56121 Pisa PI, Italy

- Estimated Cost: The price range for treatments is between €40 and €90.

2. Reflua Day Spa & Beauty
- Description: Offers a range of beauty services and spa treatments, such as skincare treatments and massages.
Via Giosuè Carducci, 16, 56125 Pisa PI, Italy is the address.
- Estimated Cost: The price range for various procedures is usually between €50 and €100.

3. Maria Rosa Estética Center
- Description: Provides moderately priced beauty services such as massages, facials, and waxing.
The address is 15 Via San Frediano, 56126 Pisa PI, Italy.
- Estimated Cost: Services range in price from €30 to €80.

4. My Place: Beautifying and Enriching
- Description: Offering affordable massages and body therapies among other spa and cosmetic services.
The address is 28 Via Sant'Antonio, 56124 Pisa PI, Italy.
- Estimated Cost: The range of prices for services is €40 to €90.

5. Center for Benessere Time Out
- Description: Provides calming surroundings and mid-range spa treatments including massages, body scrubs, and facials.
Location: Italy's 56123 Pisa PI, Via Guglielmo Marconi, 25
- Estimated Cost: The range of prices for different procedures is €50 to €110.

Expensive Beauty & Spa:
1. Pisa's Alberghi Beauty Spa
- Description: A posh spa that provides high-end services including facials, massages, and saunas.
Place of business: 32 Lungarno Antonio Pacinotti, 56125 Pisa PI, Italy
- Estimated Cost: The cost of special treatments might vary from €100 to €200 or more.

2. Grand Hotel Duomo Health Facility
- Description: A posh wellness destination providing a variety of beauty and spa services.
- Address: 94 Santa Maria Avenue, 56126 Pisa, Italy
- Estimated Cost: The range of prices for different luxury treatments is from €120 to €250.

3. Spa Bagni di Pisa
- Description: This luxurious spa is situated outside of Pisa and provides health programs, beauty treatments, and thermal baths.
Largo Shelley, 18, 56017 San Giuliano Terme PI, Italy is the address.
- Estimated Cost: Spa packages and treatments cost between €150 and €300 or more.

4. The Natural Spa & Golf Resort in Terme di Saturnia
This opulent spa complex, located outside of Pisa, provides thermal baths, aesthetic procedures, and relaxation techniques in an opulent environment.
Location: 58014 Saturnia GR, Italy; Via della Follonata
- Estimated Cost: Spa packages and treatments may be purchased for between €200 and €500 or more.

Yoga, Meditation, and Fitness Center in Pisa

Low-cost :
1. Central Palestra
- Description: Provides reasonably priced access to basic fitness center amenities, such as exercise equipment, fitness courses, and sometimes yoga sessions.

- Address: Pietro Toselli Avenue, Pisa PI, 56122, Italy
- Estimated Cost: Monthly membership fees range from €20 to €40.

2. Pilates Pisa
- Description: Offers yoga instruction at all skill levels with an emphasis on different yoga styles in a warm and inviting setting.
- Address: 56122 Pisa PI, Italy; Via Andrea Pisano, 61
- Estimated Cost: Drop-in courses cost between €8 and €15 each session.

3. Ananda Yoga Center
- Description: Provides affordable yoga lessons, meditation sessions, and seminars with an emphasis on overall well-being.
Via Carlo del Prete, 15, 56121 Pisa PI, Italy is the address.
- Estimated Cost: Classes range in price from €10 to €20 each session.

4. Palestra Pisa
- Description: For individuals looking for inexpensive exercise choices, this gym offers weight training, aerobics courses, and fitness equipment at a reasonable price.

Location: 56125 Pisa PI, Italy; Via Benedetto Cairoli, 57
- Estimated Cost: Monthly membership dues might be between €25 and €50.

5. Physical Activity
- Description: A reasonably priced fitness facility that provides a range of workout regimens, such as yoga and group fitness courses.
The address is 36 Via Montanelli, 56124 Pisa PI, Italy.
- Estimated Cost: Monthly membership fees often range from €30 to €60.

Mid-Range Cheap Yoga, Meditation, and Fitness Centers:

1. Gold's Fitness Pisa
- Description: Offers a more extensive selection of affordable exercise equipment, courses, and customized training plans.
Place of business: 68 Via Sant'Agostino, 56127 Pisa PI, Italy
- Estimated Cost: Monthly membership dues vary from €40 to €80.

2. Pisa's Yoga Loft
- Description: Provides studio-based yoga and pilates courses taught by qualified teachers with an emphasis on mindfulness and wellbeing.
- Address: 177 Via Santa Maria, 56126 Pisa, Italy
- Estimated Cost: Drop-in lessons cost between €12 and €18 each session.

3. Benessere Club
- Description: Offers wellness programs, yoga courses, and fitness workshops for holistic health at affordable prices.
- Address: Luigi Bianchi Avenue, 34, Pisa, Italy 56121
- Estimated Cost: Monthly membership fees range from €45 to €90.

4. Palestra Fitness Spazio

- Description: A reasonably priced gym that provides a variety of exercise equipment, group fitness classes, and yoga sessions for a comprehensive fitness experience.

Via Giacomo Matteotti, 24, 56124 Pisa PI, Italy is the address.

- Estimated Cost: Monthly membership dues vary from €50 to €100.

5. Pisa Ashtanga Yoga

- Description: Offers Ashtanga yoga courses that are appropriate for all skill levels and that build both mental and physical power.

Place of business: 11 Via Bonanno Pisano, 56125 Pisa PI, Italy

- Estimated Cost: Drop-in sessions often run between €10 and €20.

Luxurious Yoga, Meditation, and Fitness Facilities:

1. Pisa Bikram Yoga

This business provides intense Bikram yoga sessions that emphasize flexibility and strength in a hot atmosphere.

The address is 33 Via Chiara Gambacorti, 56125 Pisa PI, Italy.

- Estimated Cost: Drop-in lessons might cost anywhere between €20 and €30 each session.

2. Pisa's Power Yoga Studio
- Description: Offers dynamic movements and strength-building exercises during power yoga sessions.
The address is 12 Via San Martino, 56125 Pisa PI, Italy.
- Estimated Cost: Drop-in sessions range from €25 to €35 per hour.

3. Pisa Anytime Fitness
- Description: Provides yoga sessions, individualized training, and access to a state-of-the-art gym with 24-hour operation.
Location: 3, 56127 Pisa PI, Italy's Via della Fortezza
- Estimated Cost: Monthly membership dues may vary from €70 to €120.

4. Pisa, Virgin Active
- Description: A luxurious fitness facility with a wealth of facilities, one-on-one instruction, group exercise programs, and yoga sessions.
Via Gherardesca, 1, 56121 Pisa PI, Italy is the address.
- Estimated Cost: Monthly membership fees range from €80 to €150.

5. Shala Yoga Pisa

- Description: Provides mindfulness training, meditation, and classic yoga poses in a calm, upscale studio setting.

Via del Molinaccio, 7, 56124 Pisa PI, Italy is the address.

- Estimated Cost: Drop-in courses have a session fee of between €30 and €40.

CHAPTER 6: 3 AND 5-DAY PISA ITINERARY

3 Days itinerary plans

Day 1: Piazza dei Miracoli and Historical Exploration

 Morning: - 8:00 AM - Breakfast: Have a classic Italian breakfast of pastry and espresso at a neighborhood café to start your day.
Visit the famous Leaning Tower of Pisa: Leave for Piazza dei Miracoli around 9:00 AM to have a look at this iconic structure. Get tickets in advance to ascend the tower and take in the breathtaking scenery.

 Midday: - 12 p.m. - Lunch: In the vicinity of Piazza dei Miracoli, savor traditional Tuscan fare in a trattoria or café.
1:30 P.M. - Pisa Cathedral and Baptistery: Take in the architectural grandeur and historical importance of the spectacular Pisa Cathedral and Baptistery.
- 3 p.m. - Camposanto Monumentale: Take a tour of the Monumental Cemetery at Camposanto Monumentale, renowned for its calming ambiance and stunning murals.

Evening: 6:00 PM - Visit Pisa's Old Town: Take a leisurely stroll around Pisa's old town, stopping at streets like Borgo Stretto that are home to quaint cafes and stores.
- 8:00 PM - supper: Savor additional Tuscan delights with supper at a nearby trattoria.

Day 2: Unwinding and Cultural Immersion
Morning: - Go to Palazzo Blu at 9:00 a.m. Visit Palazzo Blu, an art museum that hosts a variety of exhibits and cultural activities, to start your day.

Mid-morning: 11:00 AM - Go to the Duomo Opera Museum: Discover the museum including sculptures and artworks from the Cathedral, Baptistery, and Tower, among other items from Piazza dei Miracoli.

Following: 1:00 PM - meal: Take a leisurely meal at a nearby restaurant that serves mouthwatering Tuscan fare or fresh seafood.
- 3:00 PM: Take a Tour of San Rossore Nature Park: Unwind in San Rossore Nature Park in the afternoon. Take a stroll or hire a bike to discover the stunning scenery of the park.

Evening: - 6:00 PM - supper and Relaxation: Return to the city center for supper and maybe a spa treatment.

- 8:00 PM: supper by the River Arno: Savor supper at a restaurant while taking in the picturesque surroundings of the River Arno.

Day 3: Venturing Outside of Pisa

Morning: - 9:00 AM - Lucca Day Trip: Travel only a short distance by rail or bus to the quaint town of Lucca, which is encircled by historic walls. Explore the squares, churches, and winding streets throughout the morning.

In the middle of the morning: 11:30 AM - Bike Ride around Lucca's Walls: Rent a bike and ride along the walls to get sweeping views of the town.

Afternoon: 1:00 PM - meal in Lucca: Savor the local delicacies at a charming trattoria while having a great meal.

- 3:00 PM - Return to Pisa: Spend the afternoon traveling back to Pisa.

- 4:30 PM - Visit Giardino Scotto: Take a leisurely walk around Giardino Scotto, a park by a river.

Evening: 7:00 PM - Dinner to say goodbye to: Have a spectacular goodbye meal at a recommended restaurant or trattoria to cap off your day and your time in Pisa.

You can see the finest of Pisa in three days with this itinerary, which combines historical investigation, cultural encounters, leisure, and a day excursion to adjacent Lucca. Adapt the timetable to your preferences and the attractions' opening times.

5-Days Plans for the Vacation

Day 1: Arrival and Tour of Historic Pisa

Morning: Upon arrival in Pisa, settle into your lodging and make yourself comfortable.

- 10:00 AM - Leaning Tower of Pisa: Begin your journey with seeing Piazza dei Miracoli and the famous Leaning Tower of Pisa. Scale the tower to take in the expansive vistas.

Following: 1:00 PM - Lunch: Savor a regional trattoria's Tuscan fare at Piazza dei Miracoli.

2:30 P.M. - Pisa Cathedral and Baptistery: Take a tour of this magnificent building.

Evening: - 4:30 PM - Camposanto Monumentale: Take a look at the historic artwork on display in the Camposanto Monumentale.

- 6:00 P.M. - Take a leisurely stroll along the Arno River or into the city center.

- 8:00 P.M. - Dinner: Savor a delectable meal at a well renowned pisan eatery.

Day 2: Explore Nature and Art

Morning: - Palazzo Blu: 9:00 AM Visit Palazzo Blu, an art museum with a variety of exhibits and cultural activities, to start your day.

Midmorning: - 11:00 AM - Opera House of Duomo: Discover the treasures from Piazza dei Miracoli in this museum.

Following: 1:00 PM - Lunch: Savor a leisurely meal at a café or restaurant in the area.
- 3:00 PM - San Rossore Nature Park: Take a stroll around the park or go cycling there in the afternoon.

Evening: - 6:00 PM - Leisure Time: Return to the city center for some downtime or a spa treatment.
- 8:00 P.M. - Dinner: Savor the picturesque views of the River Arno while dining at a restaurant on the river.

Day 3: Journey to Cinque Terre

Morning: - Leave for Cinque Terre at 7:30 AM From Pisa, take an early train to Cinque Terre (it takes around two hours).

Between 10:00 AM and 2:00 PM: - Discover Cinque Terre: Explore the Cinque Terre's charming towns, hiking routes, and breathtaking scenery throughout the day. Go to Manarola, Vernazza, and Monterosso.

Evening: - Leave Pisa at 5:00 PM Take a late afternoon train back to Pisa.

7:00 PM: Relaxation: Take a nap and relax at your lodging.

Day 4: Relaxation and Lucca

Morning: - 9:00 AM - Day Trip to Lucca: Travel by bus or short train to this quaint town encircled by historic walls.

Mid-morning: 11:00 AM - Lucca City Tour: Take in the city's medieval center, winding alleyways, and old buildings.

Following: 1:00 PM - Lunch: Savor a delicious meal at a trattoria in Lucca.

- 3:00 PM - Bike Ride on Lucca's Walls: Take a bike rental and ride up the city's walls to see sweeping panoramas.

Evening: Return to Pisa at 6:00 PM Return in the evening to Pisa.

- 8:00 PM: Dinner: Savor a leisurely supper at a Pisa restaurant that comes highly recommended.

Day 5: Shopping and Getting Ready to Leave

Morning: - 10:00 AM - Go shopping in Pisa to get local products and souvenirs. Check out Corso Italia and Borgo Stretto.

Following: 1:00 PM - Lunch: Try a new restaurant or savor your last meal at a favorite location in Pisa. - 3 p.m. - Packing and unwinding: Head back to your lodging to finish packing and unwind before your departure.

Evening: - 6:00 PM - Farewell: Say goodbye to Pisa and make your way to the train or airport in order to go.

This five-day plan offers a varied and fascinating holiday experience by allowing you to see the historical sites, neighboring villages, scenic splendor, and a day excursion to Cinque Terre in Pisa. Adapt the timetable to your schedule and the attractions' opening and closing times.

CHAPTER 7: PISA'S CAMPING PLANS, ADVICE, AND WEATHER

Pisa's Weather Pattern:

- Summer (June–August): Pisa has hot, dry summers with average temperatures ranging from 25°C to 30°C (77°F to 86°F). The hottest months are typically July and August, with sometimes greater temperatures. This is often a bright period with little to no rain.

Autumn (September to November): This season is characterized by moderate temperatures, with highs of 15°C to 25°C (59°F to 77°F). Though there may be more rain later in the season, it might still be nice for outdoor activities.

- Winter (December to February): Pisa has warm winters, with average highs of 41°F to 59°F (or 5°C to 15°C). Rainfall is more frequent at this time of year, however snowfall is unusual.

- Spring (March–May): Springtime temperatures are often gentler, ranging from 10°C to 20°C (50°F to 68°F). The flowers start to blossom and there are sporadic showers as the weather becomes nicer.

Ideal Time to Visit a Beach:
Summertime is the ideal time of year to explore the beaches around Pisa, especially from late May to early September. The bright, sunny weather at this

time of year is perfect for beach activities, tanning, and swimming in the Mediterranean. Nonetheless, August is always congested since it falls during the busiest travel period.

When Is Best to Do Outdoor Activities?
The greatest seasons for outdoor pursuits like hiking, cycling, and walking around the city are spring and early fall. With their pleasant temperatures and less crowds, these seasons let you enjoy outdoor activities without the scorching summer heat or the threat of torrential winter rains.

If you want to visit Pisa in the months of May through September, which are in between late spring and early fall, you may take advantage of the nice weather that is ideal for both beach excursions and outdoor exploration. Every season has its own beauty, so choose a period that suits your favorite activities and climate.

Some Advice for Pisa Camping

Selection of a Campsite:

1. Campground research: Look for campgrounds close to Pisa that meet your needs, whether they for amenities, closeness to activities, the surrounding area, or specialized services.

2. Making a Reservation in Advance: If you want to visit well-known campsites during busy times of the year, it is highly recommended that you make a reservation in advance to guarantee your spot.

Packing necessities:

3. Tents and Sleeping Equipment: Make sure you have a stable tent, sleeping pads, bags, and any other equipment you'll need for a restful night's sleep.

4. Cooking Supplies: Pack a portable stove, pots and pans, cooking utensils, and other essentials for cooking at the campground.

5. Clothes and Equipment: Bring weather-appropriate attire, such as layers for fluctuating temperatures, sturdy shoes for outdoor activities, and rain gear.

6. First Aid Kit: Always have a fully supplied first aid kit on you, complete with sunscreen, bug repellent, basic medicines, and any prescriptions you may need.

Proper Conduct when Camping:

7. Respect Nature: By picking up after oneself and without interfering with the environment, you may follow the Leave No Trace philosophy. Honor the native wildlife and plants.

8. Quiet Hours: To maintain a calm atmosphere for everyone, abide by campsite regulations, particularly those pertaining to quiet hours.

9. Fire Safety: If permitted, only create fires in approved locations, and make sure they are completely extinguished before leaving.

Safety & Safety Measures:

10. Safety precautions: Learn the location of facilities and emergency exits, as well as emergency protocols and camping regulations.

11. Weather Awareness: Keep yourself updated on the local weather and be ready for any alterations. Whenever you go camping during erratic seasons, be prepared for wind or rain.

12. Wildlife Awareness: Take note of the local fauna. To avoid drawing animals to your food, store it carefully, and observe the rules when you come across wildlife.

Looking Around:

13. Local Rules: Learn about any rules that may apply to outdoor activities including hiking, camping, and trekking. Certain places could have certain guidelines and limitations.

14. Explore Pisa and the Surrounding Areas: Enjoy hiking, bicycling, and exploring the Tuscan scenery by making the most of the neighboring sights and natural locations.

15. Cultural Etiquette: Show consideration for regional traditions, customs, and cultural landmarks while visiting the vicinity.

You may explore the grandeur of the surrounding landscapes and sights while camping near Pisa in a safe, pleasurable, and memorable way by using these camping guidelines.

Essentials for Camping in Pisa

Camping Equipment:

- Tent: A substantial tent suitable for the quantity of campers.
- Sleeping Pads & Bags: To guarantee a restful night's sleep.
- Ground Tarp and Tent Repair Kit: For future repairs and extra security.
- Table and Chairs for Camping: For lounging and eating.
- Headlamps, lanterns, and flashlights: These are necessary for nighttime visibility.
- Fuel and Portable Stove: For preparing food.
Pots, pans, and tools for preparing meals are examples of cooking utensils and cookware.
- Icebox or cooler: For the fresh storage of perishable food products.
- Multi-tool or knife: For a range of jobs and unexpected situations.
- Portable Water Filtration System: To get potable water that is pure.
- Grill or grate for cooking over a campfire: if permitted.

Clothes and Sneakers:

- Moisture-wicking apparel: Airy, lightweight apparel appropriate for warm climates.

- Hiking boots or sturdy shoes: Ideal for hiking and other outdoor activities.
- Hat and Sunglasses: For sun protection.
- Rain Gear: In the event of rain, use a waterproof jacket or poncho.
- Beach towel and swimsuit: For swimming and beach excursions.

Personal necessities:
- Personal hygiene products, such as shampoo, toothpaste, toothbrushes, and soap.
- Towel and toiletries: For ease of use, bring towels that dry quickly.
- Sunscreen and insect repellent: necessary to shield against the sun and insects.
- Personal drugs and First Aid Kit: Contains bandages and basic drugs.
- Identity and Vital Records: Store them in a waterproof sack.

Accessories for the outdoors:
- Daypack or backpack: For hiking and day excursions.
- Binoculars: For exploring or observing birds.
- Maps and guidebooks: necessary for getting about and seeing the region.
- Folding chairs or hammocks: For lounging.

Food and Hydration:
- Hydration packs or water bottles: To remain hydrated all day.
- Carry-On Water Container: Ideal for holding surplus water.
- Non-perishable food items: canned products, snacks, and meals that are simple to prepare.
- Disposable utensils, cups, and plates: For eating.

Comfort and Entertainment:
- Games, Books, or Musical Instruments: For amusement and relaxation.
- Portable speakers or radio: To listen to music while unwinding.
- Comfy items for the campsite: blankets, pillows, and sleeping mats.

Security and Emergencies:
- Basic medical supplies are included in the first aid kit.
- Emergency Contact Details: Local emergency numbers are included.
- Fire Blanket or Extinguisher: For the prevention of fires.
- Signal mirror and emergency whistle: To draw attention when necessary.
- Portable Weather Radio: To be updated on variations in the weather.

This comprehensive list includes everything you'll need for a summer camping vacation close to Pisa. Make adjustments according to the particular activities you have in mind and the length of your camping trip.

CHAPTER 8: SIMPLE LANGUAGE PHRASES TO KNOW IN PISA

Greetings

- Hello: Ciao (chow)
- Good morning: Buongiorno (bwohn-johr-noh)
- Good afternoon: Buon pomeriggio (bwohn poh-meh-reej-joh)
- Good evening: Buona sera (bwoh-nah seh-rah)
- Goodbye: Arrivederci (ah-ree-veh-dehr-chee)

Basic Phrases

- Yes: Sì (see)
- No: No (noh)
- Please: Per favore (pehr fah-voh-reh)
- Thank you: Grazie (graht-zee-eh)
- Excuse me: Scusi (skoo-zee)

Asking for Directions

- Where is...?: Dove si trova...? (doh-veh see troh-vah)
- How do I get to...?: Come arrivo a...? (koh-meh ahr-ree-voh ah)
- Is it far?: È lontano? (eh lohn-tah-noh)

- Left/Right/Straight: Sinistra/Destra/Dritto (see-nee-strah/dehs-trah/dreet-toh)

Ordering Food and Drinks

- Menu, please: Il menu, per favore (eel meh-noo, pehr fah-voh-reh)
- I would like...: Vorrei... (vohr-ray)
- Water: Acqua (ah-kwah)
- Coffee: Caffè (kah-feh)
- Beer/Wine: Birra/Vino (beer-rah/vee-noh)

Making Requests

- Could you help me, please?: Potrebbe aiutarmi, per favore? (poh-trehb-bee ahy-oo-tahr-mee, pehr fah-voh-reh)
- Could you repeat that, please?: Potrebbe ripetere, per favore? (poh-trehb-bee ree-peh-teh-reh, pehr fah-voh-reh)

Getting Around

- Where is the...?: Dove si trova il...? (doh-veh see troh-vah eel)
- Bus/Train Station: Stazione degli autobus/treni (stah-tsyoh-neh deh-lyee ah-oo-toh-boos/treh-nee)
- Taxi: Taxi (tahk-see)

Shopping

- How much does this cost?: Quanto costa questo? (kwahn-toh koh-stah kweh-stoh)
- I would like to buy...: Vorrei comprare... (vohr-ray kohm-prah-reh)

These simple phrases can help you communicate basic needs and navigate your way around Pisa more comfortably. Remember, locals appreciate any effort you make to speak their language!

CONCLUSION

As your journey through this travel guide to Pisa comes to a close, may your heart be filled with the vibrant colors of the Piazza dei Miracoli, resonating echoes of history within the walls of ancient churches, and the gentle breeze of the Tuscan landscape that whispered tales of an illustrious past.

Pisa, a city that stands proud with its iconic Leaning Tower, is not merely a place marked on a map; it's a canvas painted with architectural marvels, a treasury of cultural heritage, and a sanctuary where each cobblestone whispers secrets of a bygone era. It's a destination where the allure of the past intertwines seamlessly with the rhythm of modern life.

As you bid farewell to this enchanting city, may your memories be a mosaic of vibrant sunsets over the Arno River, the laughter echoing through bustling streets, the taste of authentic Tuscan cuisine lingering on your palate, and the warmth of the locals' hospitality ingrained in your heart.

Whether you've marveled at the Leaning Tower, wandered through the historic streets, or discovered hidden gems in its charming neighborhoods, Pisa has left an indelible mark on your journey.

Remember, dear traveler, that this guide is but a companion on your exploration. The true essence of Pisa lies in the experiences you've savored, the connections you've made, and the stories you've collected along the way.

As you venture forth from Pisa, may your spirit of adventure continue to seek the beauty and wonder that this world has to offer, carrying with you the memories and magic of this timeless city.

Farewell, dear wanderer, until the next adventure beckons you to explore new horizons.

13 Photography Tips On capturing stunning shots during Pisa Adventure using Smartphone and Digital Camera.

1. Glory of the Golden Hour: Capture the lovely light at daybreak or dusk for stunning photographs of Pisa's monuments.

2. Ingenious Composition: Experiment with unusual perspectives to give classic monuments like the Leaning Tower a new viewpoint.

3. Mastery of the Rule of Thirds: Optimize your frame by off-centering major features such as the tower for a visually beautiful arrangement.

4. Leading Lines: Use surrounding aspects to bring the viewer's attention to the primary attraction.

5. HDR for Balance: Use HDR mode in low-light situations to guarantee a well-exposed photograph with increased details.

6. Steady Shots: Reduce blur by using a tripod or a steady hand to stabilize your smartphone or digital camera.

7. Panorama Panache: Capture Pisa's grandeur by taking panoramic images that emphasize its architectural splendor.

8. Embrace Detail: Zoom in to capture fine details of buildings, highlighting textures and patterns.

9. Foreground Dynamics: Incorporate fascinating foreground objects to provide depth to your images.

10. Silhouette Magic: Experiment with silhouettes against a vivid sky, particularly at dusk.

11. Elegance in Long Exposure: Try long-exposure photographs with digital cameras to capture motion, particularly in low-light circumstances.

12. Editing Finesse: Use editing tools to fine-tune your photographs' colors, contrast, and overall visual impact.

13. Cultural Essence: Capture candid scenes of daily life in Pisa to lend a personal touch to your photography tour.

TRAVEL JOURNAL

No	Travel Location/ Place Name	Date	Rating 1-5

Thing to Carry

Clothings	Equipment	Electronic

Notes

(Friends made and Contact, Cost Calculation)

Printed in Great Britain
by Amazon